The Ten Commandments
J. I. Packer

Part Four:
DESIGN FOR LIFE,
The Ten Commandments
from *I Want to Be a Christian*

LIVING STUDIES
Tyndale House Publishers, Inc.
Wheaton, Illinois

The Ten Commandments is adapted from
I Want to Be a Christian by J. I. Packer

Fifth printing, Living Studies edition, July 1988

Library of Congress Catalog Card Number 81-86406
ISBN 0-8423-7004-8
Copyright © 1977 by Tyndale House Publishers, Inc., Wheaton, Illinois
All rights reserved
Printed in the United States of America

CONTENTS

INTRODUCTION

The motive that led me to write *I Want to Be a Christian* was to provide a textbook, or perhaps I should rather say, a resource-book, for learner groups, and also a do-it-yourself catechism course for adults who have no access to such a group. From that standpoint, this is a companion piece to my book, *Knowing God* (1972), which has been used widely for group discussion. It offers a series of quick, brief outlines—"sprints"—with questions and Bible passages for further study.

The "sprints," which are written in as compressed and suggestive a way as I can manage, are only pipe-openers, to start you talking and thinking; for anything like a full treatment of each topic, even at catechetical level, readers must go on to the questions and the Bible study.

Catechetical comes from a Greek word meaning "make to hear" and so "instruct," whence also comes *catechism* (the form of instruction), *catechumen* (the person under instruction), *catechumenate* (the organized set-up for giving instruction), and *catechize* (a verb which originally meant "instruct," though the prevalence of question-and-answer methods has given it the latter-day meaning of putting someone through his intellectual paces by interrogation). In Acts 8 we read how Philip instructed the Ethiopian eunuch; catechizing is just that process institutionalized.

Christianity is not instinctive to anyone, nor is it picked up casually without effort. It is a faith that has to be learned, and therefore taught, and so some sort of catechumenate is an essential part of a church's life.

In the first Christian centuries there was a steady stream of adult converts and enquirers, and catechetical instruction took the form of lectures, given at their level. The Reformers' strategy for revitalizing a Christendom that was ignorant of Christianity led them, however, to concentrate on a catechumenate for children. During a century and a half following Luther's pioneer *Little Catechism* of 1529, literally hundreds of catechisms were produced, mostly though not exclusively for the young, some of them official church documents, others the private compositions of individual clergymen. The English Prayer Book catechism, the Heidelberg Catechism, and the Westminster Shorter Catechism are among the best known. Probably most Protestants today associate catechisms and catechizing exclusively with nurturing children, and would not think of presentations like C. S. Lewis's *Mere Christianity*, or Billy Graham's *Peace with God*, or John Stott's *Basic Christianity*, or G. K. Chesterton's *Orthodoxy*, as catechetical, because they are written for adults. But inasmuch as they are intended to instruct outsiders and establish insiders in fundamentals of the faith, catechetical is their proper description.

One great need today is a renewal of the catechumenate for adults. It need not be called that, nor need it take the form of rigid drilling in preset formulae, which is how old-time Protestants catechized children; but somehow or other opportunities for folk in and just outside the churches to examine Christian essentials must be given, because there are so many for whom this is a prime need. Preaching does not help them, for preaching ordinarily assumes in both speaker and hearers confident certainty about the fundamentals of the faith, and where this is lacking sermons are felt to be remote and even irritating because of what appear as their unexamined assumptions. But the proper place for examining, challenging, and testing the intellectual ABCs of Christianity is not the pulpit, but rather the catechumenate—at least, so Christian history suggests.

Modern educational theory sets great store by individual exploration, personal discovery, and group discussion, and there is no reason why today's adult catechumenate should not take this form—indeed, it will be best if it does, provided we remember that Christianity has a given content and continuity, and is not an "x," an undefined quantity, to be re-invented through discussion in each new generation! C. H. Spurgeon's wicked story of the Irishman who, asked how he got on at a Plymouth Brethren meeting, said, "Oh, it was lovely; none of us knew anything, and we all taught each other," has a message for us here. It would be a libel on contemporary Brethrenism, but one has known professedly Christian groups professedly studying Christian fundamentals on which this story would make a very apt comment. Guided study groups on Christian Basics, however, such as some churches known to me run year after year, constitute a genuine and much-needed renewal of the catechumenate, and I do not expect ever to find a church that would not benefit from their introduction.

Biblical quotations, unless otherwise specified, are from the Revised Standard Version. JB is the *Jerusalem Bible*, NEB the *New English Bible*, and Phillips is J. B. Phillips.

I should like to thank the publishers for their constant encouragement, and in particular for help with the questions.

THE TEN COMMANDMENTS

And God spoke all these words, saying,

"I am the Lord your God, who brought you out of the land of Egypt, out of the house of bondage.

"You shall have no other gods before me.

"You shall not make for yourself a graven image, or any likeness of anything that is in heaven above, or that is in the earth beneath, or that is in the water under the earth; you shall not bow down to them or serve them; for I the Lord your God am a jealous God, visiting the iniquity of the fathers upon the children to the third and the fourth generation of those who hate me, but showing steadfast love to thousands of those who love me and keep my commandments.

"You shall not take the name of the Lord your God in vain; for the Lord will not hold him guiltless who takes his name in vain.

"Remember the sabbath day, to keep it holy. Six days you shall labor, and do all your work; but the seventh day is a sabbath to the Lord your God; in it you shall not do any work, you, or your son, or your daughter, your manservant, or your maidservant, or your cattle, or the sojourner who is within your gates; for in six days the Lord made heaven and earth, the sea, and all that is in them, and rested the seventh day; therefore, the Lord blessed the sabbath day and hallowed it.

"Honor your father and your mother, that your days may be long in the land which the Lord your God gives you.

"You shall not kill.

"You shall not commit adultery.

"You shall not steal.

"You shall not bear false witness against your neighbor.

"You shall not covet your neighbor's house; you shall not covet your neighbor's wife, or his manservant, or his maidservant, or his ox, or his ass, or anything that is your neighbor's."

(Exodus 20:1–17)

PREFACE

Cars are complex contraptions, and with their thousands of component parts much can go wrong. The maker's handbook, however, tells you how to get from your car a satisfying performance, with minimum wear and tear, and if you mishandle it so that it goes wrong, you cannot say that you were not warned. With the wisdom contained in the repair manual which the manufacturers also issue, the car can be mended, but as long as you pooh-pooh the maker's instructions, trouble is all you can expect.

Our cars are parables of their owners. We too are wonderfully made, complex physically and even more so psychologically and spiritually. For us, too, there is a maker's handbook—namely, God's summary of the way to live that we find in the Ten Commandments. Whether as persons we grow and blossom or shrink and wither, whether in character we become more like God or more like the devil, depends directly on whether we seek to live by what is in the Commandments or not. The rest of the Bible could be called God's repair manual, since it spells out the gospel of grace that restores sin-damaged human nature, but it is the Commandments that crystallize the basic behavior-pattern which brings satisfaction and contentment, and it is precisely for this way of living that God's grace rescues and refits us.

Suppose someone says: "I try to take the Ten Commandments seriously, and live by them, and they swamp me! Every day I fail somewhere. What am I to do?" The answer is: now that you know your own weakness and sinfulness, turn to God, and to his Son Jesus Christ, for pardon and power. Christ will bring you into a new kind of life, in which your heart's deepest desire will be to go God's way, and obedience will be burdensome no longer. That folk who take the law as their rule might find Christ the Savior as their Ruler is something to pray and work for.

God's love gave us the law, just as his love gave us the gospel, and as there is no spiritual life for us save through the gospel, which points us to Jesus Christ the Savior, so there is no spiritual health for us save as we seek in Christ's strength to keep the law, and practice the love of God and neighbor for which it calls.

Suppose people generally began to say: "By God's help I will live by the Ten Commandments every day from now on. I will set myself to honor God and obey him. I will take note of all that he says. I will be in church for worship each week. I will respect duly constituted authority, and show thanks to those to whom I owe most. I will not murder or hate. I will not commit adultery, or indulge myself in lust, or stir up lust in others. I will not steal, nor leave the path of total honesty. I will not lie or cheat. I will not envy or covet." Community life would be transformed, and massive national problems would dissolve overnight. It is something more to pray and work for.

Suppose all churches and congregations were ablaze with zeal for God, and for personal holiness, and for national righteousness—why, that would be revival! Revival is a divine visitation of communities, and its moral force is unrivaled. When God quickens his church, the tremendous purging power that overflows transforms the moral tone of society in a way that nothing else can do. That we need revival is not open to doubt; that this need should drive us to prayer cannot be doubted either.

Where the law's moral absolutes are not respected, people cease to respect either themselves or each other; humanity is deformed, and society slides into the killing decadence of mutual exploitation and self-indulgence. Living in the late 1970s, we know all about the disease. It is worth considering what it would be like to be cured. Who knows? We might even be given grace to find the prospect attractive.

1
Blueprint for Behavior

Life means relationships: with God, men, and things. Get your relationships right, and life is joy, but it is a burden otherwise. It is natural to love life, and against nature to want it to stop; yet today, as when Christianity was born, many experience life as such a meaningless misery that their thoughts turn seriously to suicide. What has gone wrong? Probably relationships. Though depression may have physical roots and yield to physical treatment, disordered relationships are usually at least part of the trouble, and for a full cure these have to be put straight.

What does that involve? Social workers know how lack of meaningful human relations wastes the spirit, and try to bring help at this point. That alone, however, is less than half the remedy. True joy comes only through meaningful relations with God, in tasting his love and walking Christ's way. This is the real *dolce vita,* the life that is genuinely sweet and good.

FORGOTTEN WISDOM

Now the blueprint for this life was set out for all time in the Ten Commandments which God gave the Jews through Moses on Sinai about thirteen centuries before Christ. Yesterday's Christians saw them as (to quote the title of William Barclay's exposition of them) *The Plain Man's Guide to Ethics.* They were right. Today's world, even today's church, has largely forgotten them (could *you* recite them?). That is our folly and loss. For here, in nugget form, is the wisdom we need.

Because Scripture calls God's Ten Commandments "law" we assume they are like the law of the land, a formal code of dos and don'ts, restricting personal freedom for the sake of public order. But the comparison is wrong. *Torah* (Hebrew for "law") means the sort of instruction a good parent gives his child. Proverbs 1:8 and 6:20 actually use "torah" for parental teaching.

Think of all the wise man's words to his son in Proverbs 1:8—8:36 as addressed to us by our heavenly Father himself (as indeed they are, as in Augustine's true phrase "what thy Scripture says, thou dost say"). That will give you a right idea of the nature and purpose of God's law. It is there, not to thwart self-expression (though it may sometimes feel like that—for children hate discipline!), but to lead us into those ways that are best for us. God's parental law expresses God's parental love.

SUB-CHRISTIAN?

Some read the Old Testament as so much primitive groping and guesswork, which the New Testament sweeps away. But "God . . . spoke through the prophets" (Hebrews 1:1), of whom Moses was the greatest (see Deuteronomy 34:10–12); and his Commandments, given through Moses, set a moral and spiritual standard for living which is not superseded, but carries God's authority forever. Note that Jesus' twofold law of love, summarizing the Commandments, comes from Moses' own God-taught elaboration of them (for that is what the Pentateuchal law-codes are). "Love your God" is from Deuteronomy 6:5, "love your neighbor" from Leviticus 19:18.

It cannot be too much stressed that Old Testament moral teaching (as distinct from the Old Testament revelation of grace) is not inferior to that of the New Testament, let alone the conventional standards of our time. The barbarities of lawless sex, violence, and exploitation, cutthroat business methods, class warfare, disregard for one's family, and the like are sanctioned only by our modern secular society. The supposedly primitive Old Testament, and the 3000-year-old Commandments in particular, are bulwarks against all these things.

But (you say) doesn't this sort of talk set the Old Testament above Christ? Can that be right? Surely teaching that antedates him by a millennium and a quarter must be inferior to his? Surely the Commandments are too negative, always and only saying "don't . . ."? Surely we must look elsewhere for full Christian standards? Fair queries; but there is a twofold answer.

First, Christ said in the Sermon on the Mount (Matthew 5:17) that he came not to *destroy* the law but to *fulfill* it; that is, to be, and help others to be, all that God in the Commandments had required. What Jesus destroyed was inadequate expositions of the law, not the law itself (Matthew 5:21–48; 15:1–9; etc.). By giving truer expositions, he actually republished the law. The Sermon on the Mount itself consists of themes from the Decalogue developed in a Christian context.

Second, the negative form of the Commandments has positive implications. "Where a sin is forbidden, the contrary duty is commanded" (Westminster Larger Catechism, question 99). The negative form was needed at Sinai (as in the West today) to curb current lawlessness which threatened both godliness and national life. But the positive content pointed up by Christ—loving God with all one's powers, and one's neighbor as oneself—is very clearly there; as we shall see.

FURTHER BIBLE STUDY

Christ and the law:
   Matthew 5:17–48; 12:1–14; 15:1–9; 22:34–40
A new life-style for new men: Ephesians 4:17—5:14

QUESTIONS FOR THOUGHT AND DISCUSSION

Why are relationships so important in our lives, and where does relationship with God fit in?

What does Packer mean in saying that Jesus "republished the law"?

The law takes the form of a series of prohibitions; yet it is held to be positive, not negative, in its content. Explain this.

2

I and You

Of the relationships which make our life, some are personal, some not. A personal relationship is with a personal subject, a "you" who says "I" when addressing us. An impersonal relationship is with a nonpersonal object, a thing, an "it." Our relations with, for instance, cars, houses, ovens, and typewriters are impersonal, even if we give them pet names; we use them as conveniences, means of expressing ourselves and executing our plans, and rightly so. But to handle persons that way is wrong and indeed destructive, for persons cannot stand being treated as things. Persons have value in themselves and are ends in themselves; they are to be respected as people, not used as pawns.

Putting it positively, persons make claims. They communicate, and ask us to communicate back. In truly personal relations each loves, honors, and serves the other, and response is the rule of life. In this fallen world, where all too often you are your god and I am mine, few relationships, even at home and with so-called friends, are personal enough; we alternately use and ignore each other dreadfully. "Nobody treats me as a person; nobody cares for me" is very much a cry of our time, but the problem is as old as mankind.

PERSONAL RELATIONS WITH GOD

Now, the Christian's relationship with God the Creator is a personal, "I-you" affair throughout. To him God is not, as he is to some, a cosmic force to harness, an infinite "it" claiming no more from him than the genie of the lamp did from Aladdin. Christians know that God has called them into a relation of mutual love and service, of mutual listening and response, of asking, giving, taking, and sharing on both sides. Christians learn this from watching and listening to God incarnate in the Gospel stories, and from noting the words of invitation, command, and promise that God spoke through prophets and apostles. And the twice-stated formula of the Commandments (Exodus 20:1–17; Deuteronomy 5:6–21) makes it particularly plain.

For the Commandments are God's edict to persons he has loved and saved, to whom he speaks in "I-you" terms at each point. "I am the Lord your God, who brought you out . . . you shall . . ." The ten directives, which embody the Creator's intention for human life as such, are here presented as means of maintaining a redeemed relationship already given by grace. And for Christians today, as for the Jews at Sinai, law-keeping (that is, meeting the claims of our God, commandments 1–4, and our neighbor, commandments 5–10) is not an attempt to win God's admiration and put him in our debt, but the form and substance of grateful personal response to his love.

We have been speaking of our Maker as if he were one person, as Jews, Moslems, and Unitarians suppose him to be; but this is the moment to point out that Christians know the one God to be tripersonal, and know too that the fellowship with the Father and the Son through the Spirit into which they, as saved sinners, are called is to be modeled on the Son's fellowship with the Father, as revealed in his life on earth. Loving obedience, joyful loyalty, and wholehearted devotion to his Father was Jesus' way; this same attitude to both the Father and the Son (and indeed the Spirit, save that we do not deal with the Spirit in the same direct manner) must now be ours. Our love-relationship to the persons of the Godhead is thus to be modeled on a love-relationship within the Godhead itself. No personal bond that any man ever knows is deeper or more demanding than this—or (be it added) has a more transforming effect.

Into all human relationships that grow, five elements enter on both sides: accepting, asking, promising, pleasing, and where necessary apologizing. Now when God takes us into his family, he accepts us through Christ's atonement; he asks for the service of our lives; his "precious and very great promises" to us (2 Peter 1:4) guarantee that we shall be protected and provided for; and he commits himself to please us by leading us into the fullness of his joy. (No apologies are ever needed for any of that!— it is all great and glorious grace.)

Our part is to accept the triune Jehovah as our God; to ask, and depend on him daily, for whatever we need; to pledge our loyal obedience, and keep our promise in his strength; to aim in all we do at pleasing him; and constantly to practice repentance, which starts with confessing and apologizing for our sins and ends with renouncing them and asking to be delivered from them. As we attend to the wishes of those we love in the human family, so we attend to the law of the Lord out of love for the Lord of the law.

The Pharisees, thinking that they did God service by lovelessly serving the law, depersonalized all relationships and dehumanized themselves, and Jesus damned them for it. Loving relations with God, and with others for his sake, are what his service, as set forth in the Decalogue, is really all about. Love responding to his love, as he declares "I am . . . you shall . . ." is the real secret of law-keeping. Have we learned this secret yet?

FURTHER BIBLE STUDY

Law-keeping with love: Deuteronomy 11
Law-keeping without love: Matthew 23

QUESTIONS FOR THOUGHT AND DISCUSSION

Why is it wrong to use people? Under what circumstances do we do it?

What is the importance of the "I-you" relationship between God and us in determining our response to the Commandments?

What does it mean to say that the Pharisees depersonalized relationships and so dehumanized themselves?

3
Law and Love

The Ten Commandments' stock is low today. Why? Partly because they are *law*, naming particular things that should and should not be done. People dislike law (that is one sign of our sinfulness), and the idea is widespread that Christians should not be led by law, only by love.

SITUATION ETHICS

This idea, for which "situation ethics" is the modern name, sees the Decalogue, with the rest of the Bible's teaching on behavior, as merely a time-honored rule of thumb (not divine teaching, but human generalizing) about ways in which love is ordinarily expressed. But, say situationists, all rules have exceptions, and the Commandments may rightly be overridden if we think we can thereby do more people more good. So in every situation the question is whether law-keeping is really the best we can do. Thus moral life becomes a jam session in which at any time I may improvise for myself rather than play the notes in the score.

Attempts have been made to justify in situationist terms actions ranging from fornication to political subversion, on the grounds of their having been done in a good cause. Situationism says that the end will justify the means.

FALSE ANTITHESIS

But the love-or-law antithesis is false, just as the downgrading of law is perverse. Love and law are not opponents but allies, forming together the axis of true morality. Law needs love as its drive, else we get the Pharisaism that puts principles before people and says one can be perfectly good without actually loving one's neighbor. The truest and kindest way to see situationism is as a reaction against real or imaginary Pharisaism. Even so it is a jump from the frying pan into the fire, inasmuch as correctness, however cold, does less damage than lawlessness, however well-meant. And love needs law as its eyes, for love (Christian *agape* as well as sexual *eros*) is blind. To want to love someone Christianly does not of itself tell you how to do it. Only as we observe the limits set by God's law can we really do people good.

Keep two truths in view. First, God's law expresses his character. It reflects his own behavior; it alerts us to what he will love and hate to see in us. It is a recipe for holiness, consecrated conformity to God, which is his true image in man. And as such (this is the second truth) God's law

24

fits human nature. As cars, being made as they are, only work well with gas in the tank, so we, being made as we are, only find fulfillment in a life of law-keeping. This is what we were both made and redeemed for.

PERMISSIVE?

Situationism is worldliness, not only because it opens the door so obviously to wayward self-indulgence, but also because it aims to squeeze Christian morality into the fashionable "permissive" mold of decadent Western secularism, which rejects the restrictions of all external authority and is sure that we are wise and good enough to see what is really best just by looking. But by biblical standards this is one of many delusions born of the satanic, God-defying pride with which we fallen creatures are all infected.

Jesus, God's Son incarnate, was the perfect man, able truly to say, "I love the Father" and "I always do what is pleasing to him" (John 14:31; 8:29). If anyone was qualified to detect shortcomings in the Ten Commandments and lead us beyond them to something better, it was he. But what did he do? He affirmed them as having authority forever (Matthew 5:18–20) and as central to true religion (19:17–19). He expounded them, showing how they forbade wrong attitudes as well as wrong actions and nailing evasions (5:21–30, sixth and seventh commandments; 15:3–9, fifth commandment; cf. 23:16–22; 5:33–36, on the principle of the third commandment). And he made a point of insisting that he kept them (Luke 6:6–10, fourth commandment). When John says, "This is the love of God, that we keep his commandments" (1 John 5:3), his words describe Jesus' own religion, as well as reminding us that Jesus defined love and discipleship to himself in terms of keeping his own commands (John 14:15, 21–24; cf. Matthew 28:19, 20). Commandment-keeping is the only true way to love the Father and the Son.

And it is the only true way to love one's neighbor, too. When Paul says that "he who loves his neighbor has fulfilled the law" (Romans 13:8; cf. 10), he explains himself by showing that love to neighbor embraces the specific prohibitions of adultery, murder, stealing, and envy. He does *not* say that love to neighbor cancels them! When my neighbor, echoing the pop song, says "Come on, let's sleep together," or sin together some other way, I show love to him (or her) not by consenting, but by resisting and showing why the suggestion should be withdrawn, as Joseph did (Genesis 39:8).

Moral permissiveness, supposedly so liberating and fulfilling, is actually wounding and destructive: not only of society (which God's law protects), but also of the lawless individual, who gets coarsened and reduced as a person every time. The first advocate of permissiveness was Satan at the Fall, but his promise of Godlikeness to the lawless was a lie. The Christian's most loving service to his neighbor in our modern world, which so readily swallows this ancient lie, is to uphold the authority of God's law as man's one true guide to true life.

FURTHER BIBLE STUDY

Love and commandments: 1 John 2, 3
Galatians 5:2—6:10

QUESTIONS FOR THOUGHT AND DISCUSSION

How do situationists justify actions which others think wrong? Do you agree with their reasoning? Can you refute it?

"Love and law are not opponents but allies." In what way?

What does God's law reveal about human nature? What help is this to us?

4
The Lord
Your God

When God gave Israel the Commandments on Sinai (Exodus 20:1–17), he introduced them by introducing himself. "God spoke all these words, saying, 'I am the Lord your God, who brought you out of . . . bondage. You shall . . .' " (verse 1ff.). What God is and has done determines what his people must be and do. So study of the Decalogue should start by seeing what it tells us about God.

First, he is the God of creation and covenant. The fourth commandment says that he made heaven, earth, sea, "and all that is in them" (verse 11). You and I and everything else exist, then, not independently, but by God's will and power. With this, the five-times-repeated formula, "the Lord (Yahweh) your God" (verses 2, 5, 7, 10, 12) reveals a covenant commitment.

"The Lord" is "Yahweh" (Jehovah), the proper name by which God wanted the Israelites to know him (see 3:15). It is from the verb "to be." God's explanation of it can be rendered "I am what (or who) I am" or "I will be what I will be" (3:13ff.), but in either case it highlights his self-existence, eternity, and sovereignty. The added words "your God," however, point to a special relationship, for which "covenant" is the regular biblical term.

COVENANT

"Yahweh" is God's covenant name, and Scripture compares his covenant to the man's commitment in marriage: a free, deliberate undertaking to love, protect, and provide for the one whom he calls "my wife" and to whom he presents himself as "your husband." "Your Maker is your husband" (Isaiah 54:5). There is no richer declaration of God's love-link with the redeemed than the simple phrase "your God," with others equally simple: "God to you" (Genesis 17:7); "I am with you" (Haggai 1:13; so said Jesus, Matthew 28:20); "God is for us" (Romans 8:31). Prepositions and personal pronouns can say a lot!

Creation and covenant together give God a double claim on our obedience. The claim springs, you might say, from both paternity (fatherhood in the sense of creatorship) and matrimony (the covenant relationship). The Creator's covenant, which in Old Testament times was for Abraham's seed through Isaac and Jacob, now embraces all who are Abraham's seed through Christ, by faith. So all we who trust Jesus Christ as our Savior must realize that, according to the covenant which Jesus mediates, God stands pledged to bless us "in Christ with every spiritual blessing" (Ephesians 1:3; cf. Romans 8:32); and obedient faithfulness to him, as our Father through Christ and our Husband in the covenant, must henceforth be the rule of our lives.

LIBERTY

Second, God is *redeemer* and *rewarder*. Redeeming means recovering from alien possession, normally by payment (thus, the old-style pawnbroker displayed with his three brass balls the sign "Redemption Office"). The God who redeemed Jews from Egyptian slavery has redeemed Christians from bondage to sin and Satan at the cost of Calvary. Now it is by keeping his law that the liberty thus secured is to be preserved.

This was true for Israel at a typical level: God told them that obedience would mean, instead of captivity, long life in "the land which the Lord your God gives you" (verse 12), as he showed "steadfast love to thousands" of those who loved him and kept his commands (verse 6). But for Israel then, as for Christians now, the deeper truth was this: that keeping God's law brings that deeper freedom (inner contentment) at which the tenth commandment tells us to aim. That is why James called it "the law of liberty" (James 1:25). Law-keeping is that life for which we were fitted by nature, unfitted by sin, and refitted by grace, the life God loves to see and reward; and for that life *liberty* is the proper name.

JEALOUSY

Third, God is *jealous,* and *judges*. His jealousy is not a moral flaw, as the word might suggest, but a moral excellence; it is the jealousy of a loyal husband who rightly desires his wife's exclusive affection. Where God's love is spurned, his will flouted, and his loyalty betrayed, he can be expected to "visit" as judge (verse 5). God speaks of those whom he thus visits as persons who, in each successive generation, "hate" him, and the verb points to the fact that deep down all who defy God's rule without being able to forget his reality do wish him dead, or different, and resent with bitter irreverence both his claims and his warnings. Can we wonder, then, or demur, when God deals with such folk in retributive judgment?

Do we reckon with God the lawgiver as he really is? "Note then the kindness and the severity of God," says Paul in Romans 11:22, speaking of the gospel; "severity towards those who have fallen, but God's kindness to you, provided you continue in his kindness . . ." Kindness and severity appear together in the Decalogue too, and we shall be wise to heed its witness to both.

FURTHER BIBLE STUDY

Covenant and commandment: Deuteronomy 29, 30

QUESTIONS FOR THOUGHT AND DISCUSSION

Why should study of the Decalogue start by examining what it says about God?

What does marriage teach us about God's covenant commitment to his people?

How does keeping God's law produce liberty?

5
Who Comes First?

The fundamental commandment, first in importance as well as in order, and basic to every other, is, "You shall have no other gods before me." True religion starts with accepting this as one's rule of life.

LOYALTY

Your god is what you love, seek, worship, serve, and allow to control you. Paul calls covetousness "idolatry" (Colossians 3:5) because what you covet—houses, possessions, ornaments, money, status, success, or whatever—is "had" as a god in this sense. To have your Maker and Savior as your God in preference to any other object of devotion (which is the point of "before") means that you live for him as his person in faithful and loyal obedience. The attitude of devoted loyalty to God, expressed in worship and service according to his Word, is that fear of the Lord (reverence, not panic!) which the Bible sees as the beginning and indeed the essence of wisdom (Job 28:28; Psalm 111:10; Proverbs 1:7; 9:10). Heart-loyalty is the soil out of which holy living grows.

OTHER GODS

What other gods could one "have" beside the Lord? Plenty. For Israel there were the Canaanite Baals, those jolly nature-gods whose worship, as we know from archaeology and Scriptures like Hosea 4:11–14, was a rampage of gluttony, drunkenness, and ritual prostitution. For us there are still the great gods Sex, Shekels, and Stomach (an unholy trinity constituting one god, self), and the other enslaving trio, Pleasure, Possessions, and Position, whose worship is described in 1 John 2:16 as "the lust of the flesh and lust of the eyes and the pride of life." Football, the Firm, Freemasonry, the Family are also gods for some, and indeed the list of other gods is endless, for anything that anyone allows to run his life becomes his god, and the claimants for this prerogative are legion. In the matter of life's basic loyalty, temptation is a many-headed monster.

CONCENTRATED LIVING

The great commandment, the first one, said Jesus, is to love the Lord your God with *all* your heart and *all* your soul and *all* your mind (Matthew 22:37; the version of these words in Mark 12:30 adds a further dimension, "all your strength"). Quoted from Deuteronomy 6:4ff., where

32

it is introduced with a reminder that the Lord is "one," meaning "the only one" (the point being, first, that none of the other gods around may be identified with him, and, second, that being the only proper claimant of our worship and service he may rightly ask for it all), this saying shows us what loyalty to God requires. It calls for love, responding to God's love in making and saving you; and it demands total concentration of purpose, so that in everything you do there is just one thing you aim at—pleasing and glorifying the Lord.

"No soldier on service gets entangled in civilian pursuits," wrote Paul, "since his aim is to satisfy the one who enlisted him" (2 Timothy 2:4). In business too, employers expect the undivided loyalty of their staff, and we think them entitled to do so. But how much stronger is God's claim! Do we give our God the resolute, wholehearted allegiance for which he asks, and which is his due? Does he really come first in our lives?

What will it mean in practice for me to put God first? This much, at least. All the 101 things I have to do each day, and the 101 demands on me which I know I must try to meet, will all be approached as ventures of loving service to him, and I shall do the best I can in everything for his sake—which attitude, as George Herbert quaintly said, "makes drudgery divine; who sweeps a room, as for thy laws, makes that and th' action fine."

And then I shall find that, through the secret work of the Spirit which is known by its effects, my very purpose of pleasing God gives me new energy for all these tasks and relationships, energy which otherwise I could not have had. "I could not love thee, dear, so much loved I not honor more," said the poet. Put "God" for "honor," and you have the deepest truth about the Christian's love of his neighbor. Self-absorbed resentments dissolve, and zest for life, happiness in doing things, and love for others all grow great when God comes first.

So wake up, enthrone your God—and *live!*

FURTHER BIBLE STUDY

Wrong priorities: Haggai 1
God despised, wearied, and robbed: Malachi 1–4

QUESTIONS FOR THOUGHT AND DISCUSSION

What characterizes whomever or whatever a person chooses for his god? What god (or God) do you serve?

Why does Packer say, "Heart-loyalty is the soil out of which holy living grows"?

What does it mean in practice to have no other gods before God?

6
Imagination

A popular song in my youth began, "Imagination is funny; it makes a cloudy day sunny . . ." Imagination is amazing! Imagination creates (think of *Lord of the Rings*, or a Shakespeare play, or a Beethoven symphony). It upholds relationships, for it shows you what the other person thinks and feels. As part of God's image in us, it is good and essential; persons without imagination are badly lacking. But, like all good things, imagination can go bad. It can be used for withdrawing from reality into fantasy, and that is wrong and ruinous. Children love make-believe, but adult relationships need realism. If one imagines other people to be different from what they are, there will be trouble, as psychiatrists and marriage counselors know all too well. And what is true of human relationships is truer still of our relationship with God.

IMAGINING GOD

How should we form thoughts of God? Not only can we not imagine him adequately, since he is at every point greater than we can grasp; we dare not trust anything our imagination suggests about him, for the built-in habit of fallen minds is to scale God down. Sin began as response to the temptation, "You will be like God" (Genesis 3:5), and the effect of our wanting to be on God's level is that we bring him down to ours. This is unrealistic, not to say irreverent, but it is what we all do when imagination is in the saddle.

Hence the second commandment, "You shall not make for yourself a graven image, or any likeness of anything." This forbids, not worshiping many gods (the first commandment covered that), but imagining the true God as like yourself or something lower. God's real attack is on mental images, of which metal images are more truly the consequence than the cause. When Israelites worshiped God under the form of a golden bull-calf, they were using their imagination to conceive him in terms of power without purity; this was their basic sin. And if imagination leads our thoughts about God, we too shall go astray. No statement starting, "This is how I like to think of God" should ever be trusted. An imagined God will always be more or less imaginary and unreal.

THE REAL GOD

Is it not maddening when, after correcting someone's wrong ideas, you find that he was not listening, and is still trotting out his old mistake? Measure by this the provocation offered to God if we fail to take note of what he has shown us of himself. For he has made a point of showing us both his hand and his heart, in his words and deeds recorded in Scripture, and supremely in the earthly life of his incarnate Son, Jesus Christ, who is in every sense his image (Colossians 1:15; cf. Hebrews 1:3; John 14:7–10). God the Father is altogether Jesus-like!—it is the most breathtaking news that anyone can ever hear. But do we attend to what is revealed? I fear not. Imagination takes over again.

What do we do? We *imagine* a clash between the presentations of God in different parts of the Old Testament, and between the entire Old Testament presentation and what we *imagine* Jesus to have been. What sort of person do you think of him as? Gentle, meek, and mild? Kind, and endlessly ready to be entreated and forgive? True—but only half the truth, and a half-truth treated as the whole truth becomes a whole falsehood. Have you forgotten how he whipped tradesmen out of the temple (Mark 11:15–17; John 2:14–16), and threw verbal vitriol at recognized church leaders (Matthew 23, etc.), and cursed the fig tree as a sign of judgment to come on unfaithful Israel (Mark 11:12–14, 20ff.)? In Jesus, as in all God's self-disclosure throughout the Bible, there is a combination of pity with purity, passion with power, and slowness to anger with severity of judgment, that should humble us to the roots of our being and move us every day to cry for mercy. But are we realists enough to see this? Or has our imagination betrayed us once again?

Do we like to think that God is light as well as love (1 John 1:5; 4:8), great and terrible as well as steadfast in love (Nehemiah 1:5)? Maybe not, but this is how he is, and woe betide us if we are foolish and inattentive enough to imagine him different.

God ends the second commandment (Exodus 20:5ff.)

by reminding us of his real nature as the *jealous* God who seeks total loyalty, the *just* God who judges his foes as they deserve, and the *gracious* God who shows "steadfast love to thousands (of generations) of those who love him and keep his commandments." And how should we keep this one? By reining in our disordered imaginations and reverently accepting that God is as he says he is. How unready and slow we are to do that! Yet we must learn to do it; for it is only as rose-colored fantasy is abandoned, and realism takes its place, that true worship—worship, that is, in truth—can begin.

FURTHER BIBLE STUDY

The golden bull-calf, and what God thought of it:
Exodus 32

QUESTIONS FOR THOUGHT AND DISCUSSION

Why cannot human imagination adequately picture God?

What is the real sin that prompts the making of images of God? Is this sin a problem in your life? What will you do about it if so?

In your own words, what is God like?

7
Are
You Serious?

"The purpose of words," said a cynical diplomat, I forget who, "is to conceal thought." As a comment on how we actually talk, this statement is too true to be good. Regularly we talk for effect, saying to each other things we do not mean and could not defend, and giving assurances which we have no firm purpose to fulfill. "Are you serious?" is a question that often needs asking, for often when we should be speaking seriously, we are not.

Reluctance to treat our word as our bond—unwillingness, that is, to count ourselves committed by what we actually said—is a symptom of sin, which is the moral maggot destroying integrity. Why are marriage vows, contracts between employer and employee, and ordinary promises— to do this, to see to that, to be here, to go there—so frequently broken? Why is our life littered with promises which, whether from malice, bad management, self-seeking, or sheer carelessness, we have failed to keep? Why do we so often let down those who trusted what we said? Because of our sinful unwillingness to take our own words seriously.

TAKING GOD'S NAME IN VAIN

The Bible, however, takes promises very seriously; God demands full faithfulness of our vows. Why? Partly because trustworthiness is part of his image, which he wants to see in us; partly because without it society falls apart. The third commandment highlights God's concern at this point.

"You shall not take the name of the Lord your God in vain," it says. "In vain" means "for unreality." What is forbidden is any use or involvement of God's name that is empty, frivolous, or insincere. This touches three things at least.

The first thing is *irreverence*, speaking or thinking of God in a way that insults him by not taking seriously his wisdom and goodness. Job offered sacrifices on behalf of his children while they were alive, for fear that they had "cursed God in their hearts" (Job 1:5); and after their deaths when his wife in her bitterness urged him, "Curse God, and die" (2:9), he would not do it. Whenever sinful self-absorption makes us hate God for what he allows to happen to us or others, we break the third commandment.

The second thing is *bad language*, using God's holy name as a swear-word to voice men's unholy feelings. Everyday profanity—for example, "Oh God," "Oh Christ," and the rest—may not be the worst of sins, but it is a nasty breach of the third commandment, since it expresses neither faith nor worship. Rage overcomes us all sometimes, and it is better, no doubt, at such times to speak violently and blasphemously than to act violently and go berserk. But if you dwell often on the truth that God is Lord and orders everything, even the frustrations, for our sanctification (Hebrews 12:5–11; cf. Romans 8:28ff.), you will find yourself able increasingly, even in the most maddening moments, to "keep your cool"—and that is best of all.

The third thing, and the one which needs special stress because, as we saw, we are all so slack here, is *promise-keeping*. If we have invoked God by name in order to give our words credence, it is monstrous irreverence if we then go back on them. "You shall not swear by my name falsely, and so profane the name of your God" (Leviticus 19:12; cf. Jeremiah 5:2; Zechariah 5:4). The Lord will not hold him guiltless who takes his name in vain.

And the point goes deeper. When Jesus attacked the Pharisees' idea that one can break without guilt any oath sworn by any sacred object, so long as God's name has not been explicitly mentioned, his point was that you cannot keep God out of any transaction; he is everywhere, and all promises are made in his presence and involve him, whether his name is mentioned or not (Matthew 5:33ff.). So all promises are sacred, and must be kept. Children know this, and feel it very strongly; it is tragic that adults should so often forget it.

The godly man, therefore, will make promises cautiously but keep them conscientiously once they are made, knowing that irresponsibility and unreliability here are great and grievous sins. How hard we find this to learn! And how much we need to learn it!

FURTHER BIBLE STUDY

Why words need watching: Matthew 12:22–37

QUESTIONS FOR THOUGHT AND DISCUSSION

Why does God demand that we keep our vows?

Does taking the Lord's name in vain have to do only with promises made in his name? Why or why not?

How would you refute the Pharisees' claim that oaths not specifically using God's name may be broken without guilt?

8
Take
My Time

The fourth commandment, "Remember the sabbath day, to keep it holy," raises questions. First, the *historical* problem: was there sabbath observance before Sinai? The word "remember" introducing the command, plus the narrative of God's earlier non-provision of manna on the seventh day because he had given it as a sabbath for rest (Exodus 16:22–30), suggests that there was, while Genesis 2:2ff. (God blessed the seventh day and hallowed it, because on it God rested) takes sabbath-keeping back to creation itself.

SABBATH & LORD'S DAY

Second, the *dispensational* problem: what is the relation between the Old Testament sabbath, the seventh day of the week, commemorating creation and redemption from Egypt (Deuteronomy 5:15), and the "Lord's day" when Christians met for worship, the first day of the week, commemorating Jesus' resurrection (see John 20:19; Acts 20:7; Revelation 1:10)? For Thomas Aquinas and the Westminster Confession, the relation is just a new way of counting six-and-one, so that Lord's day observance is the Christian form of sabbath-keeping. "From the beginning of the world to the resurrection of Christ, God appointed the seventh day of the week to be a weekly Sabbath; and the first day of the week ever since . . . which is the Christian Sabbath" (Westminster Shorter Catechism).

This seems the natural reading of the scanty evidence (i.e., the three New Testament texts noted above); but Seventh-Day Adventists continue the Saturday sabbath, denying that a change has been made, while many, with Augustine, seeing that the commanded "rest" was typical of our rest of faith in Christ, conclude that, like other Old Testament types, this commandment is now abolished. Then their reason for keeping the Lord's day is the church's traditional practice rather than God's direct command.

Third, the *ethical* problem: if the Lord's day is the Christian sabbath, how do we keep it holy? Answer—by behaving as Jesus did. His sabbaths were days, not for idle amusement, but for worshiping God and doing good—what the Shorter Catechism calls "works of necessity and mercy" (see Luke 4:16; 13:10–17; 14:1–6). Freedom from secular chores secures freedom to serve the Lord on his own day. Matthew Henry says that the sabbath was made a day of holy *rest* so that it might be a day of holy *work*. From this holy work, in our sedentary and lonely world, physical recreation and family fun will not be excluded, but worship and Christian fellowship will come first.

YOUR TIME IS GOD'S

Inferences from these three questions may be disputable, but the underlying principle is clear—namely, that we must honor God not only by our loyalty (first commandment) and thought-life (second commandment) and words (third commandment), but also by our use of time, in a rhythm of toil and rest; six days for work crowned by one day for worship. God's claim on our sabbaths reminds us that all our time is his gift, to be given back to him and used for him. "Take my life" includes "take my moments and my days—take my time, all of it." This is where true obedience to the fourth commandment begins.

That Christians are stewards of the gifts and money that God gives them is a familiar truth nowadays; that we are stewards of the time we are given is less stressed, but just as true. We can learn this from the Puritans, who often voiced their sense of the preciousness of time, and from Paul, who urges, "Look carefully then how you walk, . . . making the most of the time, because the days are evil" (Ephesians 5:15ff.; cf. Colossians 4:5). "Time" means "moment" or "opportunity"; "making the most of" is literally "buying up," "redeeming from waste or uselessness"; and the days are still "evil" in Paul's sense, namely full of temptation and opposition from satanic sources (cf. 6:11–17). Satan wants to see every minute misused; it is for us to make every minute count for God.

How? Not by a frenzied rushing to pack a quart of activity into a pint pot of time (a common present-day error), but by an ordered life-style in which, within the set rhythm of toil and rest, work and worship, due time is allotted to sleep, family, wage-earning, homemaking, prayer, recreation, and so on, so that we master time instead of being mastered by it.

Few of us, perhaps, take the fourth commandment as seriously as we should. My own failures here have been great. What, I wonder, about you?

FURTHER BIBLE STUDY

How to give time to God: Isaiah 58

QUESTIONS FOR THOUGHT AND DISCUSSION

What relation do you see between the Old Testament sabbath and the New Testament Lord's day? Defend your view against alternative views.

How can we keep the sabbath holy in our time?

Practically speaking, what is involved in giving all our time to God?

9
God and the Family

After four commandments about God's direct claims come six on what the Prayer Book Catechism calls "my duty towards my neighbour." The first of these is, "Honor your father and your mother."

RESPECT FOR PARENTS

Scripture stresses the responsibility of parents to train their children, and children to honor their parents. In the Old Testament, disrespect for parents was a major sin:

one who cursed a parent could be executed (Exodus 21:17; Leviticus 20:9), and Ham was punished for mocking his father Noah as the latter slept off the effects of potent homemade wine (Genesis 9:20–27). In the New Testament, Jesus flays the Pharisees for claiming to keep the fifth commandment while actually breaking it by leaving parents destitute (Matthew 15:3–9), and disobedience to parents betokens decadence and apostasy (Romans 1:30; 2 Timothy 3:2).

Why does God highlight the duty to "love, honour, and succour my father and mother" (as the Catechism puts it)? For many reasons.

First, the family is the basic social unit; no nation is stable or virile where family life is weak.

Second, the family is the basic spiritual unit, in which God makes parents their children's pastors and teachers.

Third, children do in fact owe their parents a huge debt of gratitude for years of care and provision.

Fourth, children need parental guidance more than they know, and impoverish themselves by rejecting it. The long life promised in Exodus 20:12 and Deuteronomy 5:16 to those who honor their parents is not guaranteed to any Christian, but it remains true that children who flout their parents suffer loss. They forfeit a degree of human maturity, and make it harder for themselves to honor a Father in heaven.

Fifth, in pre-social security days the aged had only their own children to provide for them; and even in the welfare state aging parents need their children's loving concern, just as the children once needed their parents' care.

GOD AND FAMILIES

None of this, of course, justifies parental tyrannizing or possessiveness, or requires children to bow to either. "Do not exasperate your children [and you] must not goad your children to resentment, but give them the instruction, and the correction, which belong to a Christian upbringing" (Colossians 3:21; Ephesians 6:4, NEB). Should one's parents impede one's discipleship, disobedience to parents would become a necessary evil.

But what we must realize is that God, who is himself a father—Father of our Lord Jesus Christ, and of all Christians through him—cares about families enormously. Family life, with its built-in responsibilities for both parents and children, is part of his purpose for all, and the way we behave as children and parents is a prime test of both our humanity and our godliness. Love—the caring love of parents who respect their children and want to see them mature, and the grateful love of children who respect their parents and want to see them content—is our great need here.

How urgent it is in these days that parents and children together should relearn the ways of Christian family life. In the West, yesterday's extended family has shrunk to today's nuclear family; social security and community affluence has reduced the family's importance as an economic unit; and all this has weakened family relationships. Parents are too busy to give time to their children, and young people, identifying with current "youth" culture, are more prone than ever to write off their parents as clueless old fuddy-duddies. But the fifth commandment recalls us to God's order at this point.

Honestly, now: what is, or has been, your attitude to your parents? *Honoring* them means respecting them, so to speak, for their office, their relationship to you, as we should respect clergymen and public officials, whatever we think of their personal limitations or private lives. A school contemporary of mine carved out a brilliant academic career, but grew ashamed of his parents (his father was a baker), and would not visit them or let them visit him. As in a pre-pension age the Pharisees let folk duck out of financial responsibility for parents (Jesus savaged them for it: see Mark 7:6–13), so people today duck the task of caring for parents who can no longer care for themselves. But none may claim to love their neighbor while they shrug off their parents. Some of us have some repenting to do.

FURTHER BIBLE STUDY

Pattern for families:
  Colossians 3:18–21 (cf. Ephesians 5:21—6:4)
How Jesus honored his mother:
  John 2:1–11; 19:25–27

QUESTIONS FOR THOUGHT AND DISCUSSION

Why can't a nation be strong if family life in it is weak?
How is knowledge of God's fatherhood a help to parents?
In what way is the home a testing-ground?

10
Life Is Sacred

The sixth commandment (Exodus 20:13; Deuteronomy 5:17) is "you shall not kill" (RSV) or "murder" (RV, NEB). The word signifies malicious and unlawful killing, so "murder" is more accurate. Judicial execution (e.g., for murder) and killing in war are not in view; God actually calls for both in the very books from which the commandment comes (see Exodus 21:12–17; Deuteronomy 20:10–18). However strongly we may think the death penalty inadvisable and even hateful (views vary), we may not invoke this commandment to prove our point; in its context, it has no bearing on either question, but deals with private morality.

MAN IN GOD'S IMAGE

The commandment rests on the principle that human life is holy, first because it is God's gift and second because man bears God's image (Genesis 1:27; 9:6). Human life is thus the most precious and sacred thing in the world, and to end it, or direct its ending, is God's prerogative alone. We honor God by respecting his image in each other, which means consistently preserving life and furthering each other's welfare in all possible ways.

There are several things, not always called murder, which the commandment rules out. First is *malice,* the desire to diminish someone or, as we say, to "see him dead." Jesus underlined this. "Anyone who nurses anger against his brother must be brought to judgment . . . if he sneers at him he will have to answer for it in the fires of hell" (Matthew 5:22, NEB). Hate in the heart can be as much murder as violence against the person.

Second, the commandment rules out all *cruelty* or *violence* that could weaken or shorten another person's life. It is grievous to see how crimes against the person (mugging and bombing, for instance) have increased in supposedly Christian countries, while brainwashing and interrogation by torture (and sometimes torture without the interrogation) have established themselves as standard resources of modern militarism. Had the sixth commandment been pondered, none of this would be.

KILLING THE FETUS

Third, the commandment rules out *abortion* because, as genetic science shows, the fetus is from the moment of conception a human being in process (we might say) of arriving. The fact that for several months it cannot survive outside the womb does not affect its right to the same protection that other human beings merit, and which it will itself merit after birth. Abortion can only ever be justified (and then only as a necessary evil) when the pregnancy genuinely endangers the mother's life—and, as doctors know, there are few such cases today. Legalizing abortion on other grounds is a social evil, whatever arguments of convenience are invoked.

Fourth, the commandment rules out *suicide* and *euthanasia*. Suicide (self-murder) is the act of a mind unhinged; though such acts do not of themselves forfeit God's grace, as was once thought, yet suicide is a direct breach of God's command. So is euthanasia, which is either suicide by remote control or murder based on the idea that we may lawfully "put people out of their misery" just as we lawfully shoot horses or get vets to put pets to sleep. But we may not bracket a human being with horses or pets, even if he himself in a pain-maddened moment asks us to. It is good that the law treats both suicide and euthanasia as illegal acts.

(Letting the body die when no hope of recovering consciousness remains is not, of course, euthanasia; in that case, the person must be regarded as in the most important sense dead already. The difficulty in these cases is to judge when the point at which consciousness cannot return has been reached.)

The killing of millions of Jews and cripples by the Nazis, and of millions of Russians by Russian Communists in this century shows whither denial of the sanctity of human life leads. The sixth commandment points the truer and better way.

MURDERERS

As murder storywriters assume, and as most of us learn in experience, we have in us capacities for fury, fear, envy, greed, conceit, callousness, and hate which, given the right provocation, could make killers out of us all—baby-batterers or Bluebeards, professional thugs or amateur hit men. G. K. Chesterton's Father Brown explained his method of detection by saying, "You see, it was I who killed all those people"—in the sense that he looked within himself to find the mentality that would produce the crime he was investigating, and did in fact discover it there. Chesterton lets him moralize:

"No man's really any good till he knows how bad he is, or might be; till he's realized exactly how much right he has to all this snobbery, and sneering, and talking about 'criminals,' as if they were apes in a forest ten thousand miles away . . . till he's squeezed out of his soul the last drop of the oil of the Pharisees; till his only hope is somehow or other to have captured one criminal, and kept him safe and sane under his own hat."

Brown, though fictitious, states fact. When the fathomless wells of rage and hatred in the normal human heart are tapped, the results are fearful. "There but for the grace of God go I." Only restraining and renewing grace enables anyone to keep the sixth commandment.

FURTHER BIBLE STUDY

Murder is evil: Genesis 4:1–16; 9:1–7

QUESTIONS FOR THOUGHT AND DISCUSSION

Why should hate be bracketed with murder? How do you cope with feelings of fury and hatred against other persons?

Do you agree with Packer's position on abortion and euthanasia? Why or why not?

What is the "truer and better way" that Packer refers to?

11
Sex Is Sacred

When I was very young and first met the text of the seventh commandment, I thought (believe it or not) that adultery meant simply a grown-up way of behaving. Since then I, like you, have learned that some adults do in fact see sex outside marriage as a sign of being truly grown-up—"mature" is the word used, though I think it is misapplied. (When a Sunday school pupil defined adultery as the sin of pretending to be older than you are, in moral if not physical terms, it seems to me he hit the nail on the head with a resonant bang!) But what the words "you shall not commit adultery" call us to face is, first, that sex is for marriage, and for marriage only; second, that marriage must be seen as a relation of lifelong fidelity; third, that other people's marriages must not be interfered with by sexual intrusion. One mark of true maturity is to grasp these principles, and live by them.

THE PLACE FOR SEX

Not that Scripture is squeamish about sexual joy, as Christians have sometimes been. Passages like Proverbs 5:18ff. and the Song of Songs show that God, who invented it, is all for it—in its place! But sexual activity is often out of place—when, for instance, it is directed by such motives as the quest for kicks, or for relief from mental or physical tension, or loneliness or boredom, or the desire to control or humiliate; or mere animal reaction to someone's sex appeal. Such motives cheapen sex, making it (despite the short-term excitement) trivial and ugly, and leaving behind, once the thrill is over, more of disgust than delight.

What then is the place and purpose of sex? God intends, as the story of Eve's creation from Adam shows, that the "one flesh" experience should be an expression and a heightening of the partners' sense that, being given to each other, they now belong together, each needing the other for completion and wholeness (see Genesis 2:18–24). This is the "love" that committed couples are to "make" when they mate. Children are born from their relationship, but this is secondary; what is basic is the enriching of their relationship itself through their repeated "knowing" of each other as persons who belong to each other exclusively and without reserve. So the place for sex is the place of lifelong mutual fidelity, i.e., marriage, where sexual experience grows richer as the couple experiences more and more of each other's loving faithfulness in the total relationship.

FALSE TRAILS

It follows that casual sex outside marriage (called adultery if either partner is married, fornication if not) cannot fulfill God's ideal, for it lacks the context of pledged fidelity. In casual sex a man does not strictly *love* a woman, but *uses* and so *abuses* her (however willing she may be). Nor can solitary masturbation fulfill God's ideal; sex is for relationships, not ego trips.

And the relationships intended are heterosexual only; God forbids and condemns homosexual practices (Leviticus 18:22; Romans 1:26ff.). In these days it needs to be said, indeed shouted, that accepting as from God a life without what Kinsey called "outlets" (i.e., physical sex acts) does one no harm, nor does it necessarily shrink one's humanity. After all, Jesus, the perfect man, was a celibate, and Paul, whether bereaved, deserted, or never married, lived single throughout his ministry. Not all who wish for a sexual partner can have one, but what God by circumstances calls us to he will also enable us for.

SEX IS A SIGNPOST

In the jungle of modern permissiveness the meaning and purpose of sex is missed, and its glory is lost. Our benighted society urgently needs recalling to the noble and ennobling view of sex which Scripture implies and the seventh commandment assumes: namely, that sex is for fully and permanently committed relationships which, by being the blend of affection, loyalty, and biology that they are, prepare us for and help us into that which is their archetype—"the happiness of being freely, voluntarily united" to God, men, and angels "in an ecstasy of love and delight compared with which the most rapturous love between a man and a woman on this earth is mere milk and water" (C. S. Lewis).

Will that be fun? Yes, that is one thing it will be, so no wonder God has made its earthly analogue fun too. Nor may you despise it, any more than you may deify it, on that account. The sweetness of affection between the sexes, linked (as it always is) with the sense that a couple's relationship, however complete, is never quite complete, is actually a jeweled signpost pointing us on to God. When folk in the Romeo-and-Juliet state of mind say "this thing is bigger than us," they speak more truly than they sometimes realize. But a signpost only helps those who will head the way it directs, and if you insisted on camping for life beside a lovely signpost you would be daft; you would never get anywhere.

FURTHER BIBLE STUDY

Sex mishandled: Proverbs 6:20—7:27
1 Corinthians 6:9–20
The joy of sexual love: Song of Solomon 1—8

QUESTIONS FOR THOUGHT AND DISCUSSION

What is the biblical concept of marriage? What does sex outside marriage lack in terms of God's ideal?

What is God's primary purpose for sex? What does the expression "one flesh" indicate about this?

How would you counsel a person who confessed to homosexual inclinations?

12
Stop, Thief!

"Next to your own persons and your wife, your worldly goods stand closest to you, and God means them to be secured to you, and therefore commands that no one shall take away or lessen any part of his neighbor's possessions . . . Now this is a very common vice . . . For . . . stealing signifies not only emptying chests and pockets, but also taking advantage of others at market, warehouses, wine and beer shops, workshops, in short, wherever men transact business and give money for goods and labor."

So Luther starts expounding the eighth commandment,

focusing on the principle of equity involved. Love to our neighbor requires us to hold sacred not only his person (sixth commandment) and his marriage (seventh commandment), but also his *property* and his *due*.

PROPERTY

Behind the commandment lies the Bible view of property; namely, that ownership is stewardship. By human law, my property is that which I own and may dispose of as I wish, as distinct from that which I am merely allowed to use as borrower or trustee, under conditions which the owner imposes. Bible-believers, however, know that what human law says I own—my money, goods, legal rights, and titles—I actually hold as God's trustee. In the terms of Jesus' parable, these things are *talents,* lent me by my Lord on a temporary basis to use for him. One day I shall be asked to give account of how I managed those of his resources of which I was given control.

Temptations to steal property—that is, to deprive another person of what he or she has a right to—arise because fallen man always, instinctively, wants more than he has at present, and more than others have. Blind competitiveness, expressing an equally blind jealousy, was the essence of the devil's pride when he rebelled against God, and of Cain's pride when he killed Abel (Genesis 4:4–8), and of Rebekah's and Jacob's pride when they stole Esau's birthright (Genesis 27); and it is the essence of the discontented greed condemned in the tenth commandment, which is itself the cause of the dishonest grabbing forbidden in the eighth. But it is not God's will for us to have anything that we cannot obtain by honorable means, and the only right attitude to others' property is scrupulous concern that ownership be fully respected.

WAYS OF THIEVING

No doubt this principle is both clear and commonplace.

After all, every law-code everywhere has always protected property, condemned stealing, and required damages— restitution—in the way that Scripture does (cf. Numbers 5:7; Proverbs 6:30 ff.). How else could there ever be ordered community life? It might seem that nothing here needs a second thought.

But wait. How does the principle apply? It reaches further than perhaps we realize.

There is, for instance, theft of *time*, perhaps the commonest form of theft today. Employees contract to do so many hours' work for so much pay, and fail to do it. We start late, finish early, stretch coffee, lunch, and tea breaks, and waste time in between. This is theft.

It is theft too when a tradesman fails to give *value for money*. The Old Testament damns false weights and measures (Deuteronomy 25:13–15; Amos 8:5); the modern equivalent is overpricing goods and services, cashing in on another's need. Profiteering and all forms of overcharging are theft.

Again, it is theft when *debts* are left unpaid, thus robbing the person owed of the use of money to which he is morally entitled. Letting debts hang on is a way of life for some, but Scripture condemns it. "Owe no one anything, except to love one another," says Paul (Romans 13:8). If we really love our neighbor, we shall not try to postpone paying him.

Finally, it is theft to steal a *reputation,* destroying someone's credit by malicious gossip behind his back. "Who steals my purse, steals trash," wrote Shakespeare, "but he that filches from me my good name . . . makes me poor indeed." Thus, gossip is a breach of the ninth commandment; its effect will be a breach of the eighth.

Perhaps we thought that the words "thou shalt not steal" had no relevance for us in our respectability. Perhaps we need to think again. "Let the thief no longer steal," wrote Paul (Ephesians 4:28). Could "Stop, thief!" be a word that

God is speaking to you and me?

RESTITUTION

Now be honest. We have been stirring up thoughts about ways of stealing. Has it struck you that you yourself have been stealing in some of these ways? If so, God calls you now to repent (which means, change) and make restitution to those you have defrauded. Zacchaeus, the artist in extortion, expressed his repentance by promising to restore fourfold all the money he had taken unjustly (Luke 19:8; Zacchaeus was applying the four-sheep-for-one rule of Exodus 22:1). In the Belfast revival of 1922–23, converted shipyard workers brought back tools and equipment which they had "knocked off" in such quantities that in one place an additional store shed had to be provided to hold them. That showed spiritual reality. How much reality of this kind is there about us?

FURTHER BIBLE STUDY

Thieving and cheating in the family:
Genesis 27; 29:15–30; 30:25—31:42

QUESTIONS FOR THOUGHT AND DISCUSSION

Why do you think Luther saw taking advantage of others as a form of theft?

How is stealing related to the exhortation, "owe no man anything"?

Do you agree that a man's reputation is more important than his wallet? Why or why not?

13
Truth
Is Sacred

If I call you a liar, you will feel deeply insulted, for we think of liars, persons whose word we cannot trust, as morally pretty far gone. From the ninth commandment, and much else in the Bible, we learn that this is God's estimate too. Some treat lying as a kind of fine art, but Scripture views it with horror, and our Anglo-Saxon conviction about the sanctity of truth and the shamefulness of lying reflects the Bible's health-giving influence on our culture.

FALSE WITNESS

The command not to "bear false witness against your neighbor" comes in Exodus 20:16 and Deuteronomy 5:20. The word for "false" in the first text means "untrue," that in the second means "insincere," thus pointing to the deceitful purpose which breeds the falsehood. The NEB rendering, "give false evidence," highlights the fact that the commandment relates in the first place to the law-court, where justice can only be done if witnesses tell "the truth, the whole truth, and nothing but the truth"— a formula which forcibly reminds us that exaggerations, half-truths, and misleading silences can all in effect be lies. But the principle of holding truth sacred goes beyond the law-court, and touches all our living.

WHY LIE?

Why do people lie to and about each other? Why, for that matter, did Satan ("a liar and the father of lies" according to our Lord in John 8:44) lie to Eve in the garden? Partly from malice, partly from pride. When you lie to do someone down, it is malice; when you lie to impress, move, and use him, and to keep him from seeing you in a bad light, it is pride. Satan lied (and lies) because he hates God and godly folk, and wants to extend his anti-God revolt. Men lie to shield themselves from exposure and to further their supposed interests. Wounded Jewish pride spawned false witness in court against both Jesus and Stephen (Matthew 26:59ff.; Acts 6:13). Fear, contempt, revenge, boastful conceit, fraud, and the desire to shine by telling a good story are other motives which prompt lies.

Indeed, lying in some shape or form (including "white lies," which are rarely as white as we make out) is so universal an activity as to constitute compelling proof to our fallenness, just as do the locks on all our home and car doors.

GOD AND LIES

Lying insults not only your neighbor, whom you may manage to fool, but also God, whom you can never fool. A truth-telling, promise-keeping God who "cannot lie" (Titus 1:2, NEB; also Numbers 23:19; 1 Samuel 15:29), and who wants to see in us his own moral image, naturally "hates . . . a lying tongue . . . a false witness who breathes out lies" (Proverbs 6:16–19). Lying is part of Satan's image, not God's, and we should not wonder that "every one who loves and practices falsehood" should thereby exclude himself from God's city (Revelation 22:15; cf. 21:27). There is no godliness without truthfulness. Lord, have mercy!

TRUTH AND LOVE

But when one sets out to be truthful, new problems appear. There are people to whom it is clearly not right to tell the whole truth—invalids, not yet strong enough to take bad news; enemies in wartime, to whom one should not give information, and from whom, like Rahab (Joshua 2) and Corrie ten Boom, one may have fugitives to hide; mad and bad folk, who would use what you tell them to harm others; the general public, when as a politician one is putting through a beneficent plan which depends for its effect on nobody anticipating it; and so on. Nobody doubts that in these cases responsible persons must dissemble. But does that square with the ninth commandment?

In principle, yes. What is forbidden is false witness against your neighbor—that is, as we said, prideful lying designed to do him down, and exalt you at his expense. The positive command implicit in this negative is that we should seek our neighbor's good, and speak truth to him and about him to this end. When the love which seeks his good prompts us to withhold truth which, if spoken, would bring him harm, the spirit of the ninth commandment is being observed. In such exceptional cases as we have mentioned, all courses of action have something of evil in them, and an outright lie, like that of Rahab (Joshua 2:4, 5; note the commendation of her, James 2:25) may actually be the best way, the least evil, and the truest expression of love to all the parties involved.

Yet a lie, even when prompted by love, loyalty, and an inescapable recognition that if telling it is bad, not telling it would be worse, remains an evil thing (unless, indeed, with old-style Jesuits and modern-type situationists we hold that the end justifies the means). To bear false witness for one's neighbor is not so bad as bearing false witness against him; but the lie as such, however necessary it appears, is bad, not good, and the right-minded man knows this. Rightly will he feel defiled; rightly will he seek fresh cleansing in the blood of Christ, and settle for living the only way anyone can live with our holy God—by the forgiveness of sins. Again, we say: Lord, have mercy!—and lead us not into this particular type of temptation, where only a choice of sins seems open to us, but deliver us from evil.

FURTHER BIBLE STUDY

False witness: 1 Kings 21:1–24
Acts 6:8–15
Matthew 26:57–75

QUESTIONS FOR THOUGHT AND DISCUSSION

What justification has Packer for saying that truthfulness is important not only in the courtroom, but in all life?

Why did Satan lie to Eve? Do you ever misrepresent the truth with the same motives?

Why can there be no godliness without truthfulness?

14
Be Content

In the tenth commandment, "you shall not covet," God's searchlight moves from actions to attitudes, from motions to motives, from forbidden deeds to forbidden desire. The word for "covet" conveys the thought of seeking dishonest and dishonorable gain. Coveting appears here as first cousin to envy: you see what someone else has, and you want to grab it for yourself, as Ahab wanted to grab Naboth's vineyard in 1 Kings 21. In Colossians 3:5, Paul calls coveting idolatry, because the things coveted become your god, controlling your life.

Coveting is a root of all social evil; desires that burst the bounds beget actions to match. David took Bathsheba (thus, by theft, breaking the eighth commandment) and got her pregnant (thus breaking the seventh) and then to avoid scandal arranged for her husband Uriah to be killed (thus breaking the sixth), and it all began with David coveting his neighbor's wife, in breach of the tenth (see 2 Samuel 11).

Similarly, Ahab's coveting of Naboth's vineyard next door led to the framing of Naboth by false witness (breaking the ninth commandment), his judicial murder (breaking the sixth), and his vineyard being forfeited to the crown—in other words, legally stolen (breaking the eighth).

Then there was Achan (Joshua 7; note verse 21), and also Judas, whose coveting led him to break first the eighth commandment (John 12:6) and then the sixth and ninth together as he betrayed Jesus to death by a simulated act of homage (Matthew 26:48–50), all for money (Matthew 26:14–16; cf. 27:3–5). Perhaps Paul had Achan and Judas in mind, as well as folk known to him directly, when he wrote that "the love of money is the root of all evils; it is through this craving that some have wandered away from the faith and pierced their hearts with many pangs" (1 Timothy 6:10).

CALLED TO CONTENTMENT

Put positively, "you shall not covet . . . anything that is your neighbor's" is a call to contentment with one's lot. The contentment which the tenth commandment prescribes is the supreme safeguard against temptations to break commandments five to nine. The discontented man, whose inner itch makes him self-absorbed, sees other people as tools to use in order to feed his greed, but the contented man is free as others are not to concentrate on treating his neighbor right. "There is great gain in godliness with contentment," wrote Paul (1 Timothy 6:6).

Scripture presents contentment as a spiritual secret. It is one dimension of happiness, which is itself the fruit of a relationship. Toplady focuses this superbly in a poem beginning "Happiness, thou lovely name, Where's thy seat, O tell me, where?" He writes:

> *Object of my first desire,*
>   *Jesus, crucified for me!*
> *All to happiness aspire,*
>   *Only to be found in thee.*
> *Thee to please and thee to know*
> *Constitute our bliss below,*
> *Thee to see and thee to love*
> *Constitute our bliss above.*
>
> *Whilst I feel thy love to me,*
>   *Every object teems with joy;*
> *Here, O may I walk with thee,*
>   *Then into thy presence die!*
> *Let me but thyself possess,*
> *Total sum of happiness!*
> *Real bliss I then shall prove,*
> *Heaven below, and heaven above.*

Knowing the love of Christ is the one and only source from which true contentment ever flows.

Jesus diagnosed, however, one mortal enemy to contentment: worry (see Matthew 6:25–34). But, he said, for a child of God (and every Christian is that) worry, which is in any case useless, since it can improve nothing (verse 27), is quite unnecessary. Why? Because "your heavenly Father knows" your needs (verse 32) and can be relied on to supply them as you "seek first his kingdom and his righteousness" (verse 33). Not to see this, and to lose one's contentment in consequence, shows "little faith" (verse 30). The God whose fatherhood is perfect can be trusted absolutely to care for us on a day-to-day basis. So to realize that while planning is a duty and worry is a sin, because God is in charge, and to face all circumstances with an attitude of "praise God, anyway" is a second secret of the contented life.

Nor is this all. Look at Paul, a contented man if ever there was one. From prison he wrote, "Not that I complain of want; for I have learned, in whatever state I am, to be content . . . I have learned the secret of facing . . . abundance and want. I can do all things [i.e., all that I am called to do] in him who strengthens me" (Philippians 4:11–13). The open secret to which Paul alludes here is fully spelled out in Hebrews 13:5ff.—"Put greed out of your lives and be content with whatever you have; God himself has said: *I will not fail you or desert you,* and so we can say with confidence: *With the Lord to help me, I fear nothing: what can man do to me?*" (JB). To realize the promised presence of one's loving Lord, who both orders one's circumstances and gives strength to cope with them, is the final secret of content.

DIRECTING DESIRE

We are all, of course, creatures of desire; God made us so, and philosophies like Stoicism and religions like Buddhism which aim at the extinction of desire are really inhuman in their thrust. But desire that is sinfully disordered needs redirecting, so that we stop coveting others' goods and long instead for their good, and God's glory with and through it. When Thomas Chalmers spoke of "the expulsive power of a new affection," he was thinking of the way in which knowledge of my Savior's love diverts me from the barren ways of covetous self-service, to put God first, others second, and self-gratification last in my concerns. How much do we know in experience of this divine transforming power? It is here that the final antidote to covetousness is found.

FURTHER BIBLE STUDY

From discontent to contentment: Psalm 73
Contentment in prison: Philippians 4:4–20

QUESTIONS FOR THOUGHT AND DISCUSSION

How is the contentment prescribed in the tenth commandment a safeguard against temptations to break the first nine?

Do you agree that philosophies which aim at the extinction of desire are misguided? Why or why not?

What did Thomas Chalmers mean by his phrase "the expulsive power of a new affection"?

15
Learning from the Law

What does God want to teach us today from the Commandments? Some talk as if there is nothing for modern man to learn from them, but that is not so. Though more than 3,000 years old, this ancient piece of divine instruction is a revelation of God's mind and heart for all time, just as is the nearly-2,000-years-old gospel, and its relevance to us is at least threefold.

First, the Commandments show *what sort of people God wants us to be*. From the list of prohibitions, telling us what actions God hates, we learn the behavior he wishes and loves to see. What does God in the law say "No!" to? Unfaithfulness and irreverence to himself, and dishonor and damage to our neighbor. And who is our neighbor? Jesus, asked that question, replied in effect: everyone we meet. So what does God want us to be? Persons free of these evils; persons who actively love the God who made them and their neighbors, whom he also made, every day of their lives; persons, in fact, just like Jesus, who was not only God's eternal Son but also his perfect man. A tall order? Yes, but it should not cause surprise that our holy Creator requires us to reflect his moral glory. What else could possibly please him?

THREE USES

Rightly, Reformation theology did not separate God's law from God himself, but thought of it personally and dynamically, as a word which God is continually publishing to the world through Scripture and conscience, and through which he works constantly in human lives. Spelling out this approach, Reformed theologians said that God's law has three uses, or functions: first, to maintain order in society; second, to convince us of sin and drive us to Christ for life; third, to spur us on in obedience, by means of its standards and its sanctions, all of which express God's own nature. It is the third use that is in view here.

THE LAW OF NATURE

Second, the Commandments show *what sort of life-style is truly natural for us*. Rightly have theologians understood the Commandments as declaring "natural" law, the law of our nature. This phrase means that what is commanded not only corresponds to (though going beyond) "the work of the law" written, more or less fully, on every man's conscience (see Romans 2:12ff.), but also outlines the only form of conduct that fully satisfies human nature. Deviations from it, even where unconscious, are inescapably un-fulfilling. When people shy away from the formula "God first, others second, self last," as if it were a recipe for total misery, they show that they do not understand themselves. Actually, this is the only formula that has ever brought true inward freedom and contentment on a life-long basis to anyone, and we should be glad that Christ our Master leads his disciples so firmly back to it.

People ask whether God's law binds all men or only believers. The answer is that it binds all—first, because God made us all; and second, because we are so made that without learning to obey the law we can never find the happiness and fulfillment we were made for.

There is a paradox here, which it is best not to conceal but to parade. The fulfillment of which we speak here is known only from the inside, by those who taste and see; from the outside it regularly looks to us like its exact opposite. This reflects Satan's success in persuading us, as once he persuaded Eve, that there is no fulfillment without un-restricted self-indulgence—one of the many optical illusions of the mind which he has spawned. But Jesus spoke parabolically of destroying one's own hand, foot, or eye in order to enter into life (Mark 9:43–48), and literally of forgoing marriage for the kingdom's sake (Matthew 19:12), and called all his followers to deny themselves; i.e., to be ready at his word to say "no" to anything and everything to which it would be most natural to say "yes." Can this be fulfillment? Yes—because God uses our willed detachment to attach us to himself, and fill us with himself, and that means life, light, and joy within. Christians jump into what felt to the probing toe like bitterly cold water, and find it lovely. But the world cannot discern the optical illusion, and remains skeptical.

KNOW YOURSELF

Third, the Commandments show *what sort of people we*

74

are in God's eyes—namely, lawbreakers under sentence, whose only hope lies in God's forgiving mercy. When we measure our lives by God's law, we find that self-justification and self-satisfaction are alike impossible, and we are plunged into self-despair. The producing of this effect is what the Reformers called the second use of the law. In Romans 7:7–20, Paul tells us from his own experience how it works. The law trains a searchlight on our motives and desires (Paul instances coveting), and makes us aware in ourselves of a lawless energy—you could almost call it an instinctual drive—causing forbidden motives and desires to keep bubbling up, "making me captive to the law of sin which dwells in my members" (verse 23). Thus the law, by exposing us to ourselves as spiritually sick and lost, enables us to appreciate the gospel remedy.

> *Let us love, and sing, and wonder;*
> *Let us praise the Saviour's name!*
> *He has hushed the law's loud thunder,*
> *He has quenched Mount Sinai's flame;*
> *He has washed us with his blood,*
> *He presents our souls to God!*

Hallelujah!

FURTHER BIBLE STUDY

How the law exposes sin: Romans 3:9–20; 7:7–25
How the law spurs the saint: Psalm 119

QUESTIONS FOR THOUGHT AND DISCUSSION

How do you explain the abiding relevance of the Commandments?

What does Packer mean by saying that the Commandments declare "the law of our nature"?

What do the Commandments tell you about yourself? What have you done about it, and what do you intend to do about it now?

16
The Cement of Society

So far, we have treated the Commandments as God's address to the individual ("you"), whereby he isolates us from the crowd in which our identity would otherwise be sunk and requires of us responsible personal reaction to what he says. This is a true view of them, but it is not the whole truth. For the "you" whom God first addressed in Exodus 20 and Deuteronomy 5 was Israel corporately, the nation-family which he had redeemed ("I am the Lord your God, who brought you out . . ."). And what God was teaching was his will not only for individual Israelites, but also for Israel's community life.

This too is truth for us, because it is truth for humanity as such. God made us to live in societies—family, church, body politic, the communities of business and culture—and the Commandments show God's social ideal, as well as his purpose for individuals. Indeed, the furthering of good order in society was for the Reformers, as we noted earlier, the first use of the law.

THE WAY OF STABILITY

What is God's ideal? A God-fearing community, marked by common worship (1, 2, 3) and an accepted rhythm of work and rest (4), plus an unqualified respect for marriage and the family (5, 7), for property and owner's rights (8, 10), for human life and each man's claim on our protection (6), and for truth and honesty in all relationships (9).

God's concern for communities must not be thought of as second to his concern for individuals (the way our own concern so often shapes up), for in him the two concerns are organically one. This is clear from the way in which the Old Testament repeatedly sums up his promise, which was Israel's hope, in one treasure-chest word, *shalom*. *Shalom*, translated "peace," proves when unpacked to mean, not just freedom from war and trouble, sin and irreligion, but also justice, prosperity, good fellowship, and health, and all-round communal well-being under God's gracious hand.

Modern Western Christians, who have been conditioned by their culture to wear the blinkers of a rationalistic individualism, and who are constantly being deafened by the clamor of humanists, for whom society's whole purpose is to extend the individual's range of choices, may find the unity of God's concern for the-individual-in-community and the-community-of-individuals hard to see. But that is our problem. Other generations could see it, and in Scripture the matter is clear.

So God's Commandments are in truth cement for society. It is clear that where these values are acknowledged, communities (our own, for instance, in the past) hold together, even in this fallen world; but in proportion as these values are negated, society falls apart. This can be learned both from the paganized world of injustice and revolution which was the northern kingdom of Israel (trace its sad story in 1 Kings 12—2 Kings 17, and the prophecies of Amos and Hosea), and also from the revolutions and counterrevolutions that rack the world today.

THE SECULAR STATE

Till recently most Western nations saw themselves as a continuation of medieval Christendom—that is, as social and political entities with corporate Christian commitments and ideals for living which, at least in intention, were controlled and shaped by Scripture. But now this ideal is being displaced by that of the secular state—a community that is officially without any religion or ideology save that of maximizing freedom for citizens to pursue as individuals whatever interests, religious or otherwise, they happen to have.

The change is gradual, and so the issue it raises is to some extent masked; but it is important to get it clear. Christian civilization, with its concern for the individual's health, welfare, and dignity, for integrity in public administration, and for a family life in which womanhood is honored and children's claims acknowledged, is a distinctively Christian product. Western society today is busily secularizing these concerns—that is, detaching them from their historic rootage in Christian faith, and dismissing that faith as no longer a viable basis for community life. For the moment, Western society seems so caring and compassionate that some view the secular city of today as the modern form of the kingdom of God. But, true as it is that through God's common grace good moral insights are regularly found among fallen men, Christian standards and values cannot last in a society that has corporately apostatized from Christian faith.

JUDGMENT

Why is this? Not only because denying the absolutes of faith undercuts moral absolutes too (though indeed it does), but also because moral corruption and the misery it brings are part of God's judgment on apostasy. "Since they did not see fit to acknowledge God, God gave them up to a base mind and to improper conduct," says Paul, and continues with a sample catalog of horrors that reads like a summary of the news in this morning's paper (Romans 1:28–31). Our much-vaunted "permissiveness" is actually a matter of divine curse, as was the idiotically cheerful lawlessness of Jeremiah's day. What thoughtful person can look ahead without a shudder?

What then should we say of the modern secular society? Should we see its emergence as a sign of progress? Is it not rather a sign of decadence, the start of a slide down a slippery slope with a pit at the bottom? When God's values are ignored, and the only community ideal is permissiveness, where will moral capital come from once the Christian legacy is spent? How can national policy ever rise above material self-interest, pragmatic and unprincipled? How can internal collapse be avoided as sectional interests, unrestrained by any sense of national responsibility, cut each other down? How can an overall reduction, indeed destruction, of happiness be avoided, when the revealed way of happiness, the "God first, others next, self last" of the Commandments, is rejected? The prospects are ominous. May God bring us back to himself, and to the social wisdom of his Commandments before it is too late.

FURTHER BIBLE STUDY

Dynamics of the permissive society: Romans 1:18–32
Analysis of the apostate society: Isaiah 1, 3, 5

QUESTIONS FOR THOUGHT AND DISCUSSION

Do you agree that the Commandments are meant for societies as well as individuals? Why or why not?

Does a society's attitude to the Commandments affect its future? In what way?

What replaces the Commandments in the secular state? With what result?